everyday STEM

ENGINEERING

ELECTRICAL ENGINEERING

KINGFISHER
LONDON & NEW YORK

First published 2024 in the United States by Kingfisher
120 Broadway, New York, NY 10271
Kingfisher is an imprint of Macmillan Children's Books, London
All rights reserved.

Copyright © Macmillan Publishers International Ltd. 2024

ISBN: 978-0-7534-7897-4

Distributed in the U.S. and Canada by Macmillan,
120 Broadway, New York, NY 10271

Library of Congress Cataloging-in-Publication data has been applied for.

Author Jenny Jacoby
Illustrator Luna Valentine
Series editor: Lizzie Davey
Series design: Jim Green

Kingfisher Books are available for special promotions and premiums.
For details contact:
Special Markets Department, Macmillan
120 Broadway, New York, NY 10271.

For more information please visit:
www.kingfisherbooks.com

Printed in China

9 8 7 6 5 4 3 2 1
1TR/0124/WKT/UG/128MA

EU representative: Macmillan Publishers Ireland Ltd, 1st Floor,
The Liffey Trust Centre, 117-126 Sheriff Street Upper, Dublin 1, D01 YC43

CONTENTS

ELECTRICAL ENGINEERING

Electricity can seem like magic. At the flick of a switch, light fills the room, a car will drive you across town, or you can speak to a friend on the other side of the world. But electricity is not magic—it is a natural force, and ever since scientists figured out how to create and control it, engineers have been coming up with clever and useful things to do with it. From streetlights that light your way in the dark to websites that offer you just the right video you wanted to watch, the best inventions of electrical engineering help us do more things more easily, without needing to think too much about it.

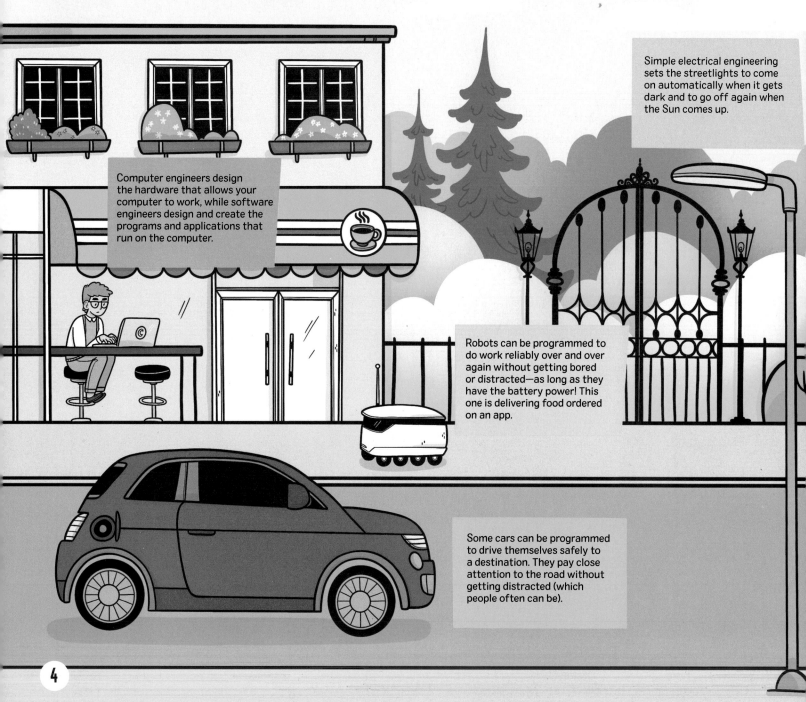

Simple electrical engineering sets the streetlights to come on automatically when it gets dark and to go off again when the Sun comes up.

Computer engineers design the hardware that allows your computer to work, while software engineers design and create the programs and applications that run on the computer.

Robots can be programmed to do work reliably over and over again without getting bored or distracted—as long as they have the battery power! This one is delivering food ordered on an app.

Some cars can be programmed to drive themselves safely to a destination. They pay close attention to the road without getting distracted (which people often can be).

Synthesizers create a huge range of different sounds by putting together different sound waves, created electronically.

Software engineers also design games! With one handheld device, each game can make the few buttons do different things, helping you jump, run, swim, and solve problems.

Electrical engineers have developed communications systems. We can now see and talk to people in real time even when they are not in the same room.

From computer animation to CGI (computer generated images), some movies can look incredibly lifelike even though they were made entirely on a computer.

Even elevators can be programmed to work intelligently. When the user calls the elevator by saying which floor they want to go to, they are sent the elevator that will get them there in the quickest time.

Electrical engineers designed headphones that can silence outside noise, leaving you to enjoy music in peace.

Software engineers develop AI (artificial intelligence) that can learn by itself and predict the things you will ask your phone to do. The electrical technology behind a touch screen is so tiny it's called "nanotechnology."

DID YOU KNOW?

The world's first electric streetlights were introduced in London in 1878. Before that, the lights were gas flames and lamplighters would have to light each one by hand every evening.

WHAT MAKES AN ELECTRICAL ENGINEER?

Electrical engineers need to know all about the science behind electricity—where it comes from, how it can be made to flow, and how to control it. They use math to check whether their circuits will safely carry the amount of electricity that will flow through it. There are a lot of special extra parts that can be added to electrical circuits that each do a small job. When electrical engineers have learned all the facts, skills, and safety rules, they can begin to be creative!

1. Every project starts with an **idea**. Engineers look around to find a problem or something that could be improved and then think up ways they might solve it using the knowledge they have. Then they use logic to figure out how to put together an electric circuit or program that could solve that problem.

Sketching out an idea can be a good way to develop ideas for an invention.

Electricity is always engineered in a **circuit**. It can only keep flowing and powering a device if it works in a continuous loop.

"Breadboards" are used to try out (or "prototype") an electric circuit, to check that all the right components have been included. The parts can be plugged into holes in the board and easily taken out again, so you can try and try again until it works just right.

Inventions don't work perfectly the first time. **Mistakes** tell you what things to make better next time.

All electric systems need **power**. It can come from a battery or from a power outlet in a wall.

2. Engineers try out an idea and then figure out how to improve any part of the system that doesn't work or that could work better. By **trying, improving, and trying again,** they end up with a new, helpful invention. Mistakes are the best way for engineers to find out how to improve their creations.

SAFETY!

Because electricity can be very dangerous, all electrical engineers learn how to work with it safely. Anything that uses electricity has to be made completely safe for people to use. If any of the live electrical wires can reach a person, it can be very dangerous—the electricity can flow through the body. A little electricity feels like a tingle. A bigger amount can give an unpleasant shock. A large amount of electricity can be deadly.

Sharing ideas with teammates can help solve problems before you get started.

3. Different electrical engineers have different skills, so engineers often **work as a team**. Some people are great at coming up with ideas. Others love to build something and then try it out, fix problems, and make improvements. Teams also need a leader, to make sure everyone knows what job they are doing and that they have everything they need to work well.

When you are happy your circuit idea works as a prototype and you know you want the circuit to last, the components can be soldered onto a **circuit board**.

4. Because engineers invent stuff, it's important that there are inventions to help all the **different people** in the world and all their different needs. No one group of people can invent everything for everyone, so it's really important that all types of people become electrical engineers.

WHAT IS ELECTRICITY?

Electricity is a form of energy. It comes from the buildup of electrons, which are tiny parts of an atom that have a small electrical charge. Electricity exists in nature, but it wasn't until the 1830s that a scientist named Michael Faraday discovered a way to make it start flowing through wires. Knowing how to generate and harness electricity is the first step in electrical engineering.

MAKING ELECTRICITY FLOW

Electrons have a negative charge. Negative forces are attracted to positive forces, so electrons will flow toward anything with a positive charge. Electric engineering organizes this electrical charge to flow safely through a circuit of wires—this is why batteries have a positive end and a negative end. Electricity will only flow in a circuit, and power is needed to make it flow. As the current flows, it can power various devices that are part of the circuit.

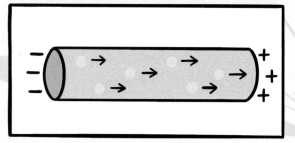

MICHAEL FARADAY'S INVENTION

A few scientists in the early nineteenth century had shown that electricity and magnetism were linked, and they had used electricity to create a magnetic field. In 1831 Michael Faraday became the first person to use electromagnetism the other way: by using magnets to create electricity. He built a machine that rotated a magnet inside a coil of wire and found that electricity started to flow inside the wire. Today most electricity is still generated in this way, using powerful turbines to turn magnets inside large coils of wire.

INSULATORS AND CONDUCTORS

Electricity will only flow through certain materials, called conductors. Metals are excellent conductors, which is why electrical wires are metal (usually copper).

Other materials, called insulators, don't let electricity pass. Plastic and rubber are insulators, which is why electrical wires are coated in plastic. The different colored coatings also help engineers know what job each wire is doing.

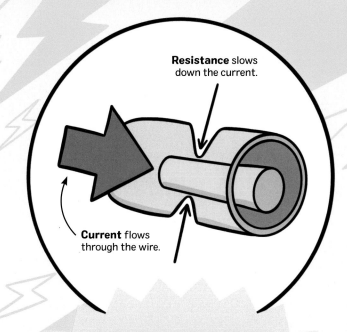

Resistance slows down the current.

Current flows through the wire.

MEASURING ELECTRICITY

There are three different electrical measurements that engineers need to know:

Current (measured in amps) is the flow of electricity—how much charge is traveling across one point in the circuit every second.

Resistance (measured in ohms) is the force that slows down the electrical current. Some materials offer resistance by conducting electricity while slowing it down a bit.

Voltage (measured in volts) is the pressure that sends electricity around a circuit. The bigger the current and the resistance, the bigger the voltage.

ELECTRICITY IN NATURE

Wherever electrons build up, you might see electricity. Lightning happens when so many electrons have built up in clouds high in the sky that they are desperate to reach the ground. The charge jumps from the cloud to the earth, giving off a loud bang and a burst of light. In the earth, the negative charge is neutralized. The burst of noise and light shows that electricity can be very powerful—and dangerous! You might also notice static electricity if you rub a balloon on your hair and find your hair sticking up. This is because the charged electrons have transferred onto your hair and are trying to repel each other, making your hair wave around.

ENGINEERING ELECTRICITY

Electrical engineering starts off with a circuit. The circuit must include a power source (such as a battery), a device, and wires to connect everything up in a closed loop. There are many different parts (called "components") that can be added into a circuit to do different jobs.

SYMBOLS

Because electricity can be dangerous, it is vital that engineers designing and building circuits communicate clearly. Engineers use a language of symbols to make it very clear what is to be used at each step. Electrical engineers draw a circuit map to plan their ideas before they start making any electricity flow. Not only is this safer, but it helps them figure out where something might have gone wrong when they're testing it out.

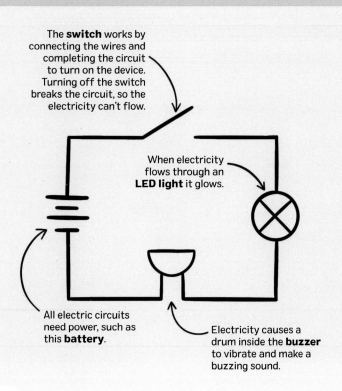

The **switch** works by connecting the wires and completing the circuit to turn on the device. Turning off the switch breaks the circuit, so the electricity can't flow.

When electricity flows through an **LED light** it glows.

All electric circuits need power, such as this **battery**.

Electricity causes a drum inside the **buzzer** to vibrate and make a buzzing sound.

THE COMPONENT TOOLBOX

A multimeter is used to measure different electrical values in a circuit: the voltage, the current, and the resistance.

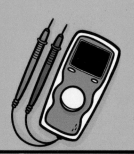

A battery—or several batteries used together—is one way of powering electricity. Some devices can also be plugged into the domestic power supply through an outlet in the wall.

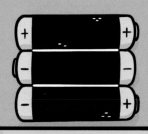

When building an electrical circuit, it can be useful to use different **colored wires** to keep track of which wire leads where. However, the color doesn't make a difference to the work the wire does—the wire is the same inside.

LED lights look fun but are also a good way of showing whether electricity is flowing through a circuit.

Alligator clips make it easy to connect different components to a circuit. The red clips usually connect to the positive end of the battery or component, and the black clips to the negative end.

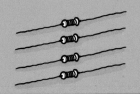

Resistors can be added to a circuit to reduce the flow of electricity through the circuit. Too much electricity at once can cause a circuit or one of its components to burn out.

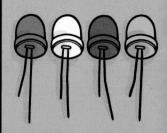

A capacitor stores energy in a circuit. It builds up electrical energy quickly while the current flows and can then let go of its energy quickly too. It is useful for powering things such as camera flashes and lasers.

Diodes only let current flow in one direction. Depending on the way it is put into a circuit, a diode can block the current or allow it to flow.

Transistors are like switches that can switch the electric current on and off and help amplify (increase) the current already flowing. They can turn parts of an electronic circuit on and off or direct more electricity to a different part of the circuit.

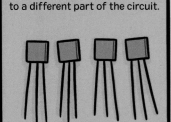

A potentiometer is a slider or dial that changes the resistance in a circuit. The change of resistance can control different things, such as the volume of a speaker or a joystick in a video game.

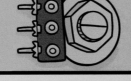

A switch can start and stop the electricity flowing in a circuit by breaking or connecting the circuit.

A breadboard is a place to connect components in a circuit without needing to solder parts in place, so each part can easily be added in or adjusted.

AYAH BDEIR
(BORN 1982)

Born in Canada and raised in Lebanon, Ayah Bdeir grew up playing with chemistry sets and taking things apart to see how they worked. After studying computer engineering and sociology in Beirut, and earning a master's degree in media arts and sciences at the Massachusetts Institute of Technology, she created littleBits—electronic building blocks for children to play with and create simple electronics.

Ayah's mission is to help children understand the workings behind the electronic devices that form such an important part of our lives.

POWER

Electricity has always been part of people's lives. Throughout history, people have witnessed the power of electrical storms and "played" with static electricity. However, it wasn't until the nineteenth century that scientists learned how to use electricity to power useful devices, such as light bulbs. At first, most electricity was made to provide light—because the darkness had always limited what people could do, and electric light is much safer than candles or gas. In the modern world, electricity brings us ever more reliable power, allowing us to use it for more and more useful things.

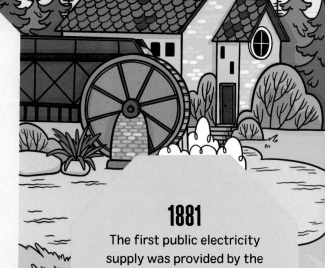

1881
The first public electricity supply was provided by the first power plant, built in Godalming, England. It was powered by a water wheel.

1800
Alessandro Volta invented the first battery, called the "voltaic pile."

1879
Thomas Edison patented the first commercially available light bulb.

Electricity is measured in volts (named for Alessandro Volta).

1831
Michael Faraday discovered electromagnetic induction, creating electricity with magnets and wires.

1890s

Technology improved to transmit electricity over longer distances, using alternating current (AC) and transformers. A battle began between AC and DC, to see which would be most used for public electricity supplies.

1939

Britain creates the world's first national power grid, with most homes across the country linked up to it.

1882

Thomas Edison built the world's first steam-powered electricity power plant, providing the world's first large-scale electric power network, in New York City. It provided direct current (DC).

AC AND DC

With direct current, electricity flows in one direction around the circuit. This is the original way electric circuits were designed, and it is how small, battery-powered devices work.

With alternating current, the electricity flows in one direction for a short time, then switches direction, so each electron will only travel back and forth over a short distance. AC can send higher voltages over longer distances than DC.

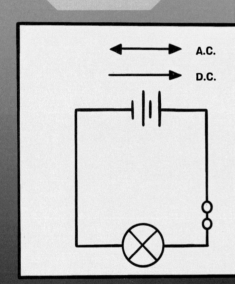

A.C.

D.C.

TODAY

So much electricity is used today that satellite images show the world lit up at nighttime.

NATIONAL ELECTRICITY GRIDS

A national electricity grid is a way of sending electricity across a whole country. It is a network of cables that carry high-voltage electricity from power plants, where it is generated, to substations, where the voltage is reduced so it can be safely sent to homes and other buildings.

National electricity grids are useful because the whole country can benefit from power being generated in different areas. International grids are even more useful! Morocco has a lot of solar farms and can export power to neighboring countries. Norway does the same with hydroelectric power.

FUTURE

Satellites keeping a view over Earth may be able to react to conditions on the ground and control national and international power systems.

COMMUNICATIONS

As soon as people had discovered how to generate an electric current, engineers began looking for ways to use electricity to communicate across long distances. They first did this in the 1840s, with the telegraph. That invention allowed people to communicate instantly, rather than waiting weeks for a horse and buggy to deliver a letter.

In the 1800s, linemen set up hundreds of thousands of miles of telegraph wire. In the U.S. this helped open up the West to settlers from the East.

HOW TELEGRAPHS WORK

Telegraph wires can travel huge distances, but they work like any simple electric circuit. This includes a receiver that makes a noise (like a buzzer) and a key, which acts like a switch. Each time the operator presses the key, it completes the circuit, and the buzzer makes a sound at the other end. Invented alongside the telegraph was a way of turning buzzing sounds into messages.

In Morse code, each letter of the alphabet is given a code of a combination of dots and dashes. By pressing the telegraph key briefly for a dot and a bit longer for a dash, coded messages can be sent. Morse wasn't the only code used in telegraphs, but it is the one most remembered today.

HOW A TELEPHONE WORKS

The telephone system took over from telegraphs. Telephone receivers were a technological upgrade, because they could transform electrical signals into a wider range of sounds than a single buzz. The microphone turns the sounds spoken into the in the mouthpiece into pulses of electrical current. The pattern of current travels down the phone wire to the person listening at the other end, where the pulses are changed by the phone speaker into sounds that the listener can hear.

NIKOLA TESLA
(1856-1943)

Nikola Tesla was a Serbian inventor who later became an American citizen. He was famous for demonstrating his electrical inventions with great showmanship, and he invented the induction motor, which was vital in sending an electricity supply across long distances.

Nikola wanted to invent a way to transmit electricity without using wires. He invented the Tesla coil. In this coil, so much electric charge builds up that when it discharges it can leap across air to a conductor—like man-made lightning. This invention was used in some medical equipment and radio transmitters. It also provides a fun and shocking display at museums around the world.

Nikola set his final dreams on finding a way to transmit radio waves over long distances, but he was beaten to the invention by Guglielmo Marconi.

GUGLIELMO MARCONI
(1874-1937)

Guglielmo Marconi was an Italian inventor who beat Tesla to inventing a wireless telegraph system, which became the radio system that is still used today.

Guglielmo was born into a rich family. He did not go to school but was fascinated by science and electricity, and he was able to build his own equipment to make experiments and test out his ideas.

Instead of using pulses of electricity through wires to transmit information, Guglielmo figured out how to use radio waves and send them over long distances. His first demonstrations, in England, sent radio waves across 3.7 mi. (6 km). He won the Nobel Prize for Physics in 1909.

IN YOUR POCKET

In our pockets we can carry around everyday objects that make daily life easier than ever. We can pay for things, find our way, listen to music, and communicate with people all over the world. These items are so useful that it is easy to forget that they contain some extremely clever electrical engineering and computer power, shrunk down to a tiny scale.

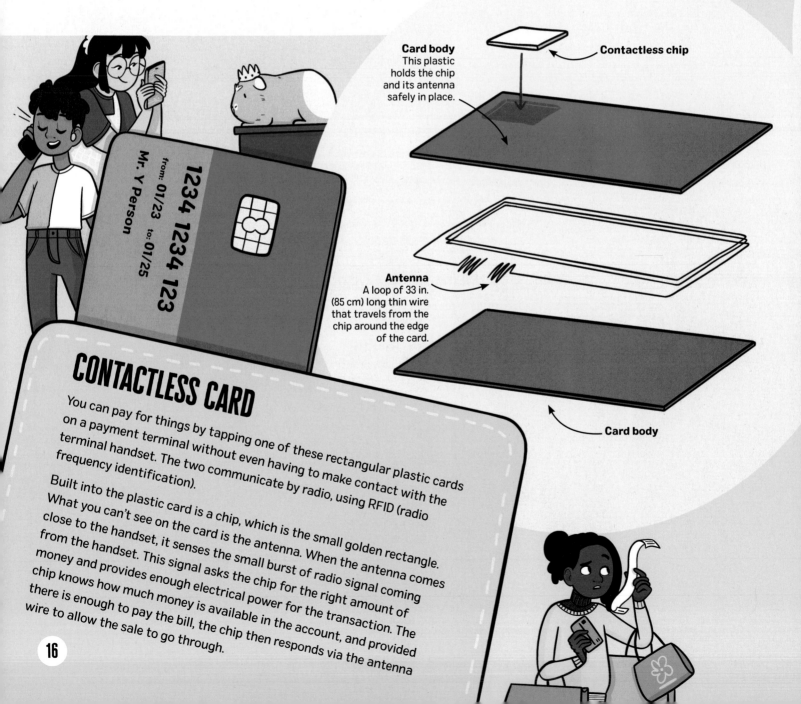

Contactless chip

Card body
This plastic holds the chip and its antenna safely in place.

Antenna
A loop of 33 in. (85 cm) long thin wire that travels from the chip around the edge of the card.

Card body

1234 1234 123
from: 01/23 to: 01/25
Mr. Y Person

CONTACTLESS CARD

You can pay for things by tapping one of these rectangular plastic cards on a payment terminal without even having to make contact with the terminal handset. The two communicate by radio, using RFID (radio frequency identification).

Built into the plastic card is a chip, which is the small golden rectangle. What you can't see on the card is the antenna. When the antenna comes close to the handset, it senses the small burst of radio signal coming from the handset. This signal asks the chip for the right amount of money and provides enough electrical power for the transaction. The chip knows how much money is available in the account, and provided there is enough to pay the bill, the chip then responds via the antenna wire to allow the sale to go through.

The **system-on-a-chip (SOC)** is only about the size of a penny, but it is extremely complex! It contains between 5 and 10 billion tiny transistors (components that control which way the electricity flows in a circuit).

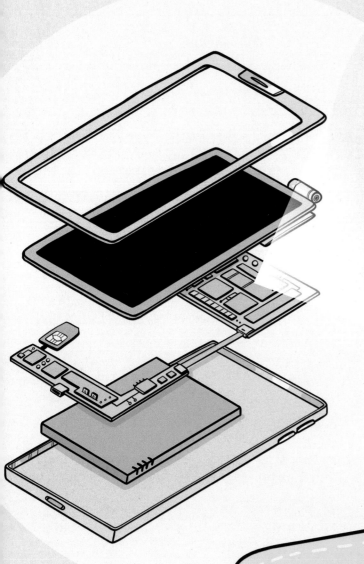

DID YOU KNOW?

Smart watches do most of the things a smartphone can do, with some extra benefits from being strapped to your wrist. Being close to your body at all times, the watch can monitor your body temperature, heart rate, and even blood oxygen. It could even alert you early if you might be getting sick.

SMARTPHONE

There are many different parts inside the workings of a smartphone. The **flash memory** holds all the things that people tend to store on their phone to look at or listen to frequently, such as photos, songs, and contacts. The **dynamic random access memory** is like the thinking part of the phone and does all the live bits of working while you're using the phone. The **system-on-a-chip** (SOC) is a network that connects all the different parts together. Different areas within the SOC do yet more things, such as working with graphics, remembering things, working with the speaker and microphone, and interpreting instructions from the touch screen. It also holds the part that connects to the Internet via WiFi and Bluetooth.

ON THE STREET

When you go out and about on the streets on foot, by bicycle, bus, or car, electrical engineering helps keep you safe. It helps you see in the dark and keeps you safe from other road users. Some electrical devices take advantage of being out on the street all day and use the Sun to charge their solar panels.

STREETLIGHTS

Components in electric circuits control streetlights so that the lights only come on in the dark. A light-dependent resistor (LDR) works like a switch. As the amount of light falls, the resistance in the LDR reduces, allowing the electricity to flow—and the light comes on.

TRAFFIC LIGHTS

Traffic lights tell each lane of traffic when it can go or when it has to wait to let other traffic or pedestrians pass. The stop/go settings used to be programmed to change after a set amount of time, but traffic light controls now react to when vehicles and pedestrians are waiting to cross.

ELECTRIC CAR

Electric cars run on batteries, so we need to charge them up from time to time. Some streetlights have been adapted so that electric cars can plug into the light and draw electricity from the same source as the streetlight.

YVETTE STEVENS

Yvette Stevens was Sierra Leone's first female engineer. She rose from being a village technical expert to Sierra Leone's first ambassador to the United Nations.

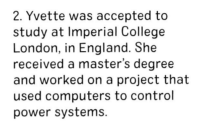

1. Stevens was born in Sierra Leone at a time when girls weren't taught much science in secondary school. She became one of just two girls studying in the final two years of a boys' school.

2. Yvette was accepted to study at Imperial College London, in England. She received a master's degree and worked on a project that used computers to control power systems.

3. Yvette returned to Sierra Leone in 1974 and became the country's first female engineer. She taught at the university and designed systems for buildings. She researched technology to help people, particularly women, in rural areas.

4. Yvette's experience led her to the UN, where she helped highlight technology that would aid people in developing countries. At the UN High Commission for Refugees, she helped use solar energy to provide power at refugee camps.

5. Yvette created the first energy policy for Sierra Leone and oversaw solar-powered street lighting in the country's regional capitals.

6. In 2012, Yvette became Sierra Leone's first ambassador to the UN. She used her position to champion women in the UN's scientific organizations.

ENGINEERING AND THINKING LOGICALLY HAS BEEN ESSENTIAL TO MY SUCCESS.

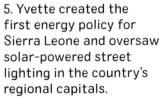

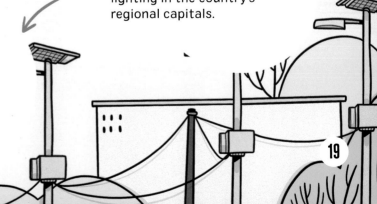

IN YOUR HOME

Many of the machines in your home make your life easy without your even noticing. Many domestic machines work so cleverly because they are controlled by electrical engineering and computer programs.

Alarm clock
A digital clock keeps time using a quartz crystal oscillator. When electricity is sent to a thin piece of quartz crystal in an oscillator, the crystal changes shape slightly. Changing shape makes the crystal vibrate, and each vibration sends a signal. The clock mechanism knows how many signals show that a second, minute, or hour has passed.

Range hood
Electricity powers a fan, which sucks air through a filter into the hood. The filter clears out much of the smoke, grease, and cooking smells before either sending the air back into the room or through some pipes to the outside.

Induction stove
Within this stove is a coil of wire. When electricity passes through, it creates a magnetic field. Only a pan with a magnetized base will heat up here and be able to cook food. The stove doesn't get hot, so it is safe to touch.

Washing machine
When you fill the washing machine with your dirty clothes, you need to select a program to instruct the machine. The program starts by letting water pour into the drum. A thermostat measures the temperature of the water. When it's hot enough, the drum starts turning, moving the clothes around. Then it drains the water and repeats the rinsing and draining. Finally, the drum spins fast so the water is pulled out of the clothes.

Oven clock
A quartz crystal oscillator helps this clock with timekeeping and can count down cooking time.

Electric toothbrush

Inside an electric toothbrush is a motor that is powered by a small electric circuit and a rechargeable battery. As the motor spins around and around, it moves a crank from side to side. The crank is attached to the brush head, so it makes the brush move from side to side very fast, cleaning your teeth quickly and effectively.

Ground source heat pump

The house is heated by a ground source heat pump. Pipes buried about 5–6.5 ft. (1.5–2 m) underground are filled with a liquid that absorbs the heat from the earth. The liquid travels indoors, where a compressor increases its temperature, and then the warm pipes transfer their heat to the home's heating system. A thermostat measures the temperature of the room and controls the output of heat to keep the air at a steady temperature.

Electric meter

Meters record the amount of electricity used in the home over a period of time. Each meter monitors the electricity flowing through the wire that brings in the electricity supply for all the appliances used in the household.

Smoke detector

This smoke detector works by detecting smoke particles that rise up on hot air from a fire. Inside its detection chamber is an electric circuit that contains a photocell and an alarm. If light falls on the photocell, it makes electricity flow, which sets off the alarm.

ELECTRICAL ENTERTAINMENT

Computer engineering has revolutionized sports and entertainment. New developments in what cameras and technology can do have made it possible to solve arguments in sports. On screen, we can now create the illusion of whole new worlds out of pure imagination combined with technical know-how.

GREEN SCREEN

By filming in front of a green screen, moviemakers can make actors look like they're in places or situations that would be too dangerous, impractical, or expensive to actually film in. During the editing process, the editor can tell the software to take out anything green and replace it with the new background. This could be something filmed elsewhere—perhaps by a drone flying over mountains or a canyon—or scenery created by CGI. Actors wearing green suits can be made to look like they're in entirely other bodies!

HAWK-EYE

This technology is used to track the path a ball takes in various sports. In tennis, it uses ten cameras positioned around the court to follow the ball's journey and accurately say whether the ball bounced inside or outside a line. In soccer, seven cameras monitor each goal and alert the referee when the ball has definitely bounced inside the goal. The cameras are also useful for doctors and physiotherapists, as they can see exactly what happened to any injured players.

DIY ENTERTAINMENT

Apps for smartphones and tablets have made it easy and fun for people to create their own music and animations at home. The hard work of coding and programming is done by the app designers so that the user can choose sounds to connect together into loops of music, or animate their own drawings by clicking together simple commands.

ELECTRONIC MUSIC

People experimented with ways of making music with new electronic devices from the late nineteenth century, but it wasn't until the 1950s and '60s that synthesizers began to take off. The word "synthesize" means to put together. Synthesizers work by putting together different electronic tones to make sounds that can sound either like recognizable instruments or like something completely new. Originally synthesizers were huge pieces of equipment, but now they can be small and portable, or even part of programs on a laptop or tablet.

HOW SYNTHESIZERS WORK

Like any musical instrument, synthesizers need an input. This is the instruction to make a particular note. The input on a synthesizer is usually a keyboard, like on a piano.

Synthesizer sound is created in the oscillator. To oscillate means to move in a steady rhythm, and the sound comes out in a steady pitch. It can then be adjusted by other parts of the synthesizer.

Synthesizers have dials that adjust the volume, shape, or tone of the sound. These are called envelopes and filters. They control things such as how quickly the loudest part of the note occurs and when it starts to fade. Here are some of the different sounds a synthesizer can make:

White noise sounds like heavy rain or the roar of traffic, and the wave looks like a scribble.

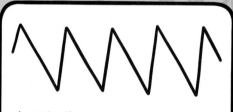

A **sawtooth** wave sounds harsh and buzzy.

Sine waves give a simple, slightly muffled sound.

A **triangular** wave is brighter and cleaner than a sine wave and less harsh than a sawtooth wave.

ELECTRONIC MUSIC TIME LINE

1919: Theremin This is played by moving your hands around near the antennae, but without touching them. The hands change the electromagnetic field around the antennae, changing the sounds.

(1956): RCA Electronic Music Synthesizer Mark 1 This was one of the first programmable synthesizers, and it was huge—it took up a whole room at Columbia University!

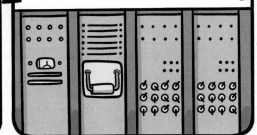

1964: Moog modular synthesizer The first synthesizer that was produced for people to buy included a keyboard for the input.

Today: laptop and mouse Music can now be made electronically without buying hardware or instruments, using special software on a personal computer.

1983: Yamaha DX7 One of the most popular digital synthesizers, this created new sounds that changed the sound of popular music in the 1980s.

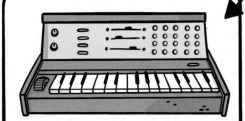

1970: Minimoog This was the first affordable, portable synthesizer.

WENDY CARLOS (1939–)

Wendy is a pioneer of electronic music. She met Robert Moog in the 1960s, when he was developing his first synthesizer, and advised him on ways to make it best suit a composer and performer. She changed public attitudes toward synthesizers by creating *Switched-On Bach*—an album of Bach's music recreated with a Moog synthesizer, in 1968. Wendy had to work a lot harder to make the music than synthesizer users do today, as only one note could be played at a time and it was difficult to keep the music in tune. Her patience paid off: *Switched-On Bach* was the first classical music album to sell a million copies.

THE INTERNET

The first time two distant computers communicated with each other was in 1969. However, their connection was so flimsy that only the letters "LO" made it onto that first email. Modern technology has improved enormously, and so many people around the world now have their own personal computers and smart devices that by 2020 there were 4.7 billion people using the Internet worldwide.

THE WORLD WIDE WEB

Today most people access the Internet by looking at websites hosted on the World Wide Web. Website information is translated into electronic signals, which travel through wires, or wirelessly by WiFi. The information is then translated back into the words, pictures, audio, and video we see.

This translation is done using **network protocols**. The network protocols all follow the same set of rules, so a user can communicate with the Internet whatever the type of machine they are using.

TIM BERNERS-LEE (BORN 1955)

Tim was born in London, England, in 1955. His parents were both computer scientists, and as a child he learned electronics by playing with his model train set.

Tim studied physics at University of Oxford. As a student, he bought an old TV from a repair store and turned it into a computer.

In 1980 Tim started working at a research center. His job was to develop a computer language so the computers used by the 10,000 researchers there could "talk" to each other. He invented a hypertext language called ENQUIRE. Hypertext is language that is linked to the original text being sent, but separate from it.

By 1989 Tim had the idea to build the World Wide Web, a "web" of hypertext documents viewed in a browser using the Internet. The Internet and the hypertext documents already existed—Tim's World Wide Web would link the two. In 1990 Tim published the first website on the first web browser, which he built. The first public web browser was released in 1991. The World Wide Web took off rapidly, because it was freely available for everyone to use.

ALGORITHMS

Computers are great because they do complicated things that would either be too difficult or take too long for most people to do. Computers don't get numbers mixed up or accidentally write down the wrong answer. However, computers can usually only do what we ask them to. One of the ways we program computers is with algorithms.

ALGORITHM RECIPE

An algorithm is a step-by-step way of solving a problem. Algorithms are used in programs to help computers break down complex problems into smaller steps that are easier to solve. Each step needs to be very clear so that the instruction can be followed exactly.

You could think of a recipe as an algorithm. By following each step exactly, you will end up with the right result—hopefully a tasty meal! But if any of the steps are not written clearly enough, you could go wrong and end up with a cake that doesn't rise or a dish that tastes disgusting.

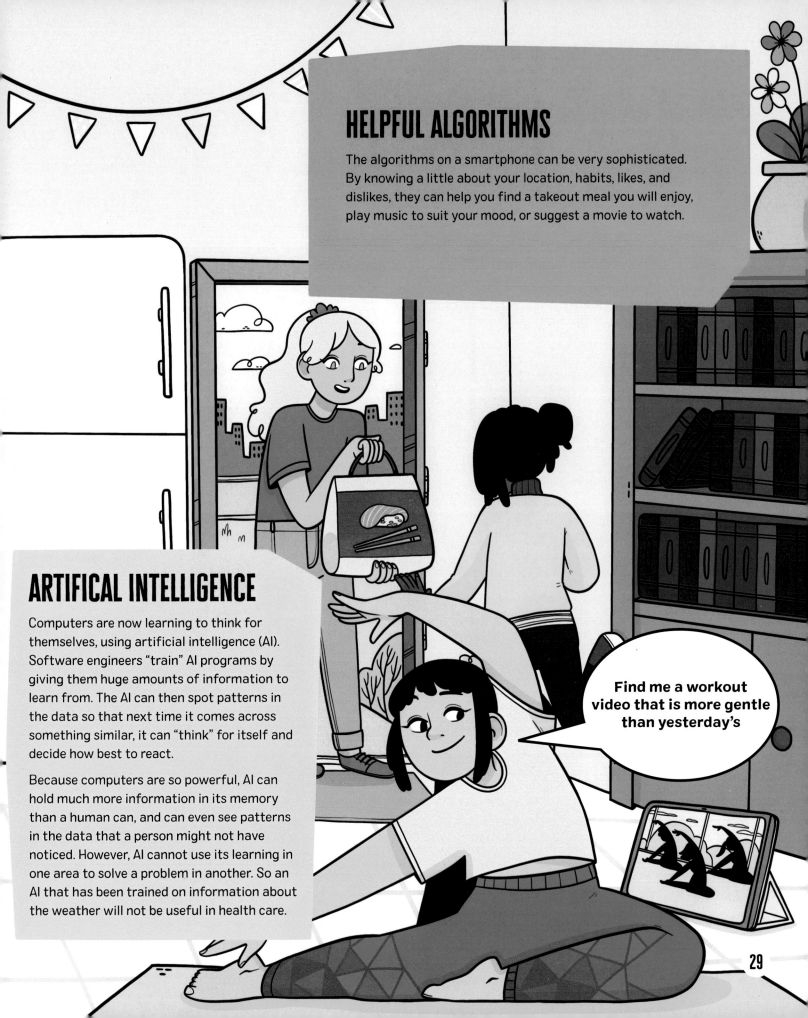

HELPFUL ALGORITHMS

The algorithms on a smartphone can be very sophisticated. By knowing a little about your location, habits, likes, and dislikes, they can help you find a takeout meal you will enjoy, play music to suit your mood, or suggest a movie to watch.

ARTIFICAL INTELLIGENCE

Computers are now learning to think for themselves, using artificial intelligence (AI). Software engineers "train" AI programs by giving them huge amounts of information to learn from. The AI can then spot patterns in the data so that next time it comes across something similar, it can "think" for itself and decide how best to react.

Because computers are so powerful, AI can hold much more information in its memory than a human can, and can even see patterns in the data that a person might not have noticed. However, AI cannot use its learning in one area to solve a problem in another. So an AI that has been trained on information about the weather will not be useful in health care.

Find me a workout video that is more gentle than yesterday's

29

MOBILE COMMUNICATIONS

Cell phones are important to people everywhere. There are well over 5 billion cell phone users around the world, which is almost two-thirds of the world's population. It is hard to believe, but more people have a cell phone than have access to a safe toilet. Phones don't just mean an easy way to have a chat with a friend. All kinds of useful tools and information can be quickly shared across cell networks.

MONEY TRANSFERS

Cell phones allow people to send and receive money, even when they live far away from banks or ATMs. If someone has a wallet on their phone, they can use the phone itself to pay for things. Or someone can send money by phone and someone else can pick it up as cash at a collection point. This is popular in places where a family member might move away to the city and want to send money home to the countryside.

FARMING HELP

Smartphones help farmers ensure that their crops receive just the right amount of water they need—and without them needing to leave their home! Sensors placed in the fields can monitor the moisture in the ground, as well as how much rain, wind, and light the crops are receiving at any moment. The farmer can check this information and use a remote control to let just the right amount of water flow onto the field.

SMART HOMES

Apps on a smartphone can control your home environment so you don't waste energy. On a cold day, you can use an app to let your home heating system know what time you will get home and it will get ready for your return—so you don't waste electricity heating up an empty house. On a hot, sunny day, smart shutters on windows could sense the light and heat and close up automatically, keeping indoors cool.

PACEMAKERS

Each heartbeat starts with an electrical pulse. As it travels around the heart, it makes different parts of the heart contract in a particular rhythm. Each contraction pushes the blood around the body. If a person has a condition in which the heart doesn't always pump in the right rhythm, doctors can insert a pacemaker. Leads are inserted into the chambers of the heart. As soon as the pacemaker notices that the heart has slowed down or skipped a beat, it sends a small electrical pulse down the wires to bring the heartbeat back to normal.

BLOOD SUGAR MONITORS

The body is always monitoring the amount of glucose flowing in the blood ("blood sugar") and keeps it at a set level. It is dangerous for the body to have too much or too little.

When a person has diabetes, their body can't control their blood sugar, so a monitor can help. The monitor sits on the belly or arm, with a tiny sensor going under the skin to measure the amount of glucose surrounding the cells. When there's too much or too little, the monitor beeps an alert.

ELECTRIC HEALTH

Electrical engineering can help keep us healthy, because the human body is powered by electricity! Here are some inventions that tap in to the electricity in our bodies to help keep us well or make us better.

SPEEDING HEALING

When we have a wound, we might cover it with a Band-Aid. Scientists know that putting a small electrical field around the wound can help it heal. One day there might even be bandages embedded with materials that can generate a small amount of electricity, to help the wound heal more quickly.

PAIN RELIEF

It sounds odd that pain can be relieved by giving the body small electric shocks, but this is what a TENS machine does. It sends small pulses of electricity through electrodes stuck onto the skin around the area that hurts. The electricity helps reduce the pain signals going to the brain.

CANCER

A high voltage of electricity can be sent directly into a tumor to kill off certain cancers. Traditional cancer treatments often cause a lot of side effects because the medicine affects the whole body. Targeting just the tumor cells with electricity is a good way of controlling the disease without making the patient ill.

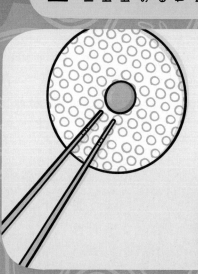

WEATHER

Predicting the weather is very complicated. Weather is affected by things that don't change much, such as the oceans, landscape, and tilt of Earth, as well as by things that change all the time, such as the seasons, pollution, and amount of radiation coming from the Sun. Supercomputers help us monitor and predict the weather—and they do it better than humans can alone. They collect measurements from weather stations all around the world and then use mathematical models to do thousands of calculations per second to predict what the weather will be like over the next few hours, days, and weeks.

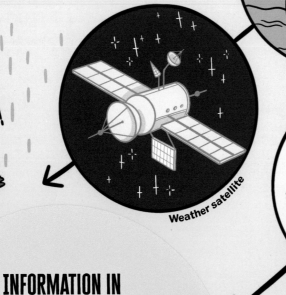

Weather balloon

Weather buoy

Weather radar

Weather satellite

Weather station

INFORMATION IN

Supercomputers collect information (called data) recorded by satellites in space, weather balloons traveling through the sky, buoys floating on the sea, and weather stations in all different kinds of locations. The more locations the information comes from, the more accurately the supercomputers can predict the weather. The information collected includes temperature, wind speed, wind direction, and air pressure.

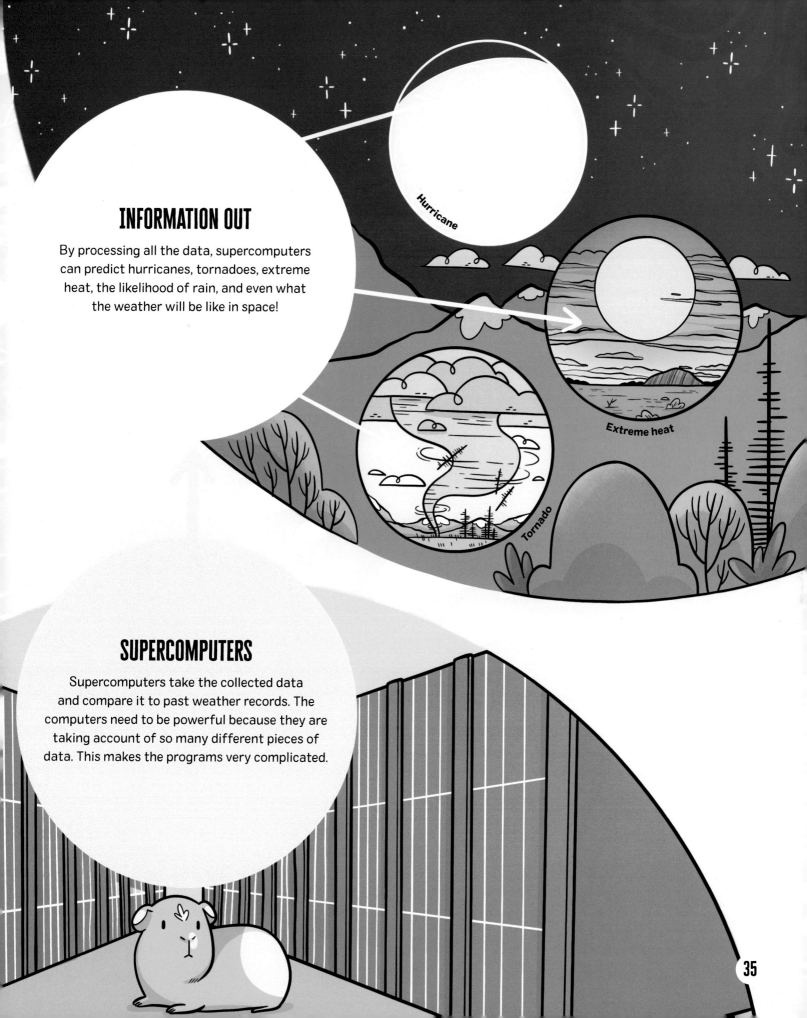

INFORMATION OUT

By processing all the data, supercomputers can predict hurricanes, tornadoes, extreme heat, the likelihood of rain, and even what the weather will be like in space!

Hurricane

Extreme heat

Tornado

SUPERCOMPUTERS

Supercomputers take the collected data and compare it to past weather records. The computers need to be powerful because they are taking account of so many different pieces of data. This makes the programs very complicated.

ELECTRIC TRANSPORTATION

Electrical engineering is even helping to improve the way our transportation systems work and is making modes of transportation better for the environment.

ELECTRIC CARS

Electric vehicles (EVs) are better for the environment than those run on gasoline because they are much less polluting. One difficulty with EVs is that you can't travel as far on a fully charged battery as you could on a tank full of gas in a traditional car. Another problem is that car batteries contain toxic materials, and they are hard to recycle. Engineers are working on improving car batteries so that they charge more quickly, last for longer trips, and can be made from less toxic materials.

FLIGHT

Air travel is one of the most polluting forms of transportation, and it contributes heavily to climate change. Engineers trying to make electric-powered flight have already managed to build small electric planes that can make short flights. Small planes and short flights are the most environmentally damaging, and it is hoped these flights may become electric soon. With electric planes the skies would be cleaner and quieter.

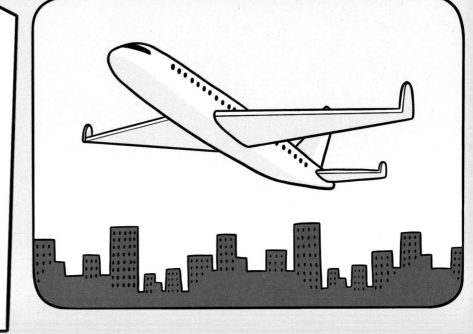

TRACTOR-TRAILERS

It is hard to make batteries for big vehicles such as tractor-trailers. One idea that could help in the future would be a lane on the Interstate specifically for these trucks, with overhead power cables that the trucks could tap in to. This would power the Interstate stretch of a truck's drive, leaving its batteries fully charged for the shorter parts of its trip.

ROUTE FINDING

Apps can help drivers navigate a route. They receive information from satellites and other users about how much traffic is on certain roads, or if traffic is not flowing as it should. They then suggest a route to the driver that takes all this live information into account, making the trip as efficient as possible.

FUTURE ELECTRICITY

Lives everywhere are completely reliant on electricity—from the alarms that wake us in the morning to the lights we see by in the dark. But the majority of electricity around the world is created by burning fossil fuels, which are polluting and create greenhouse gases that contribute to climate change. To protect our planet we need to change how we produce electricity. The good news is that green electricity is becoming more common, and exciting new ideas for making it are being developed.

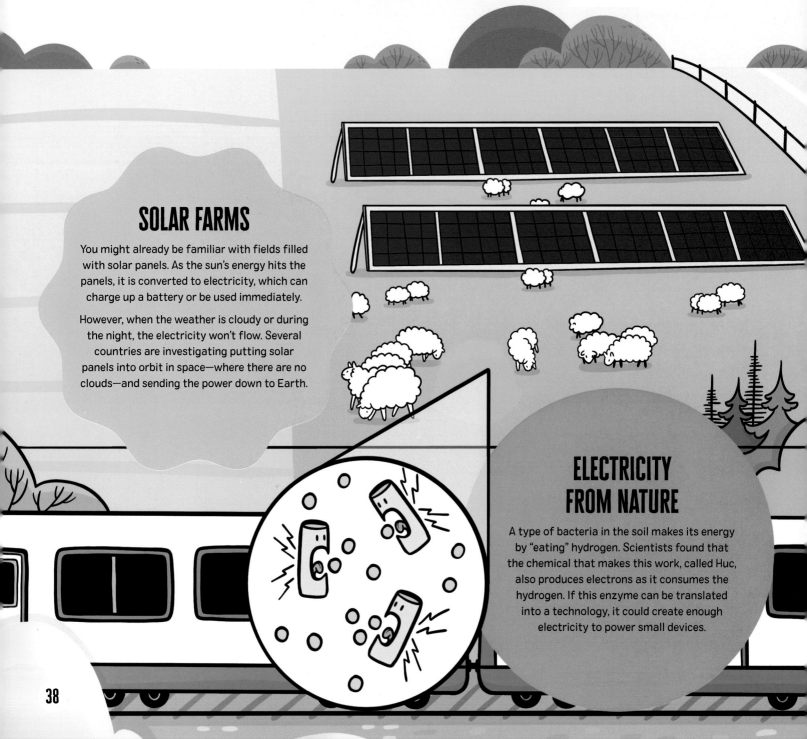

SOLAR FARMS

You might already be familiar with fields filled with solar panels. As the sun's energy hits the panels, it is converted to electricity, which can charge up a battery or be used immediately.

However, when the weather is cloudy or during the night, the electricity won't flow. Several countries are investigating putting solar panels into orbit in space—where there are no clouds—and sending the power down to Earth.

ELECTRICITY FROM NATURE

A type of bacteria in the soil makes its energy by "eating" hydrogen. Scientists found that the chemical that makes this work, called Huc, also produces electrons as it consumes the hydrogen. If this enzyme can be translated into a technology, it could create enough electricity to power small devices.

STORING ELECTRICITY

Some of these technologies produce electricity only at certain times—when the sun is shining or the wind is blowing—but the power can be stored in batteries. Batteries usually contain materials such as lithium, which needs to be mined from underground, and mining can destroy the environment. Also, there is only a limited amount of these chemicals. Engineers are busy researching batteries that use much more common chemicals, such as sodium, which is found in table salt.

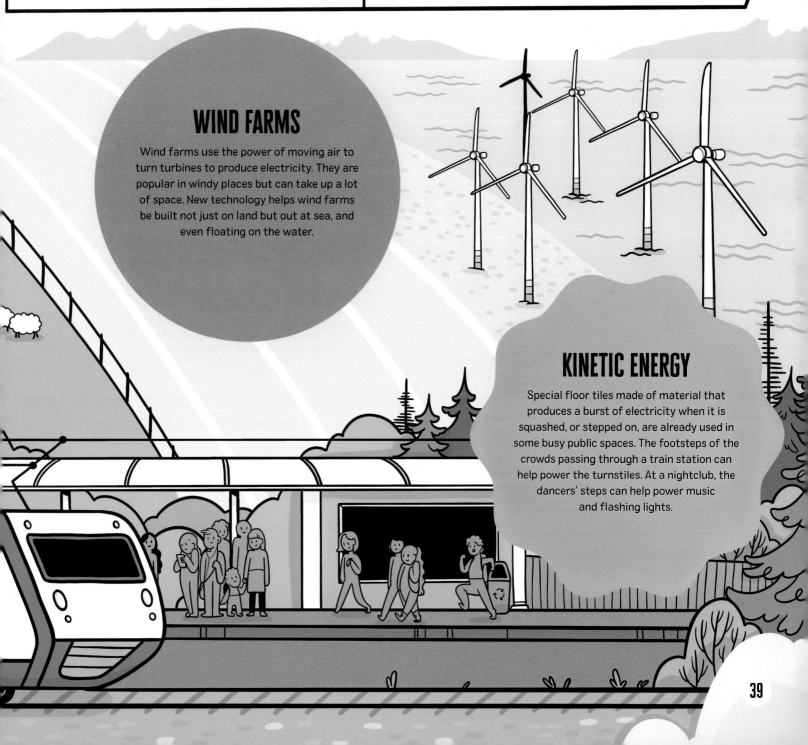

WIND FARMS

Wind farms use the power of moving air to turn turbines to produce electricity. They are popular in windy places but can take up a lot of space. New technology helps wind farms be built not just on land but out at sea, and even floating on the water.

KINETIC ENERGY

Special floor tiles made of material that produces a burst of electricity when it is squashed, or stepped on, are already used in some busy public spaces. The footsteps of the crowds passing through a train station can help power the turnstiles. At a nightclub, the dancers' steps can help power music and flashing lights.

ELECTRICITY TEST

If you have an old flashlight that isn't needed anymore, you could turn it into a machine to test materials for conductivity.

YOUR TURN!

YOU WILL NEED

- Three pieces of wire (you could take these from an old electronic device you no longer need, such as an old phone charger—but ask an adult first!)
- Scissors
- Wire strippers (or scissors will work)
- A flashlight (you will be taking this apart, so ask permission first!)
- Batteries—use the number and type that were used in the flashlight
- A collection of household objects, such as silverware, paper clips, aluminum foil, a wooden spoon, coins

You may also need
- Screwdriver
- Rubber bands

INSTRUCTIONS

1. First, cut three pieces of wire, each 4 in. (10 cm) long. If you need to take the wire from an old device, cut the wire and remove the insulating rubber cover (often colored white), to reveal three smaller wires.

2. Ask an adult to use scissors or wire strippers to take off about 0.5 in. (1 cm) of the colored insulation at each end of the wires so that the metal part is exposed.

3. Open up the flashlight, remove the batteries and on/off switch, and unscrew the part that holds the bulb. You might need an adult to help.

4. Find the + and – ends of the battery or battery pack, and use electrical tape to attach the metal end of one wire to the + end, and the end of another wire to the – end. Make sure the metal parts make good contact.

5. Now take the other ends of the two wires and connect them to the two metal contacts on the bulb house. The bulb may need the wire coming from the + end of the battery to connect to the – end of the bulb, and vice versa. If you can't tell which part of the bulb is + or – try it out one way, and if it doesn't work, swap it over. The bulb should light up. If not, try out the troubleshooting ideas.

6. When the bulb lights up, you have a working circuit. Next, add a third wire, so you can test other materials for conductivity. Untape the wire from one end of the battery and replace it with the end from the third wire. Because the circuit is now open, the bulb should have turned off.

7. Pick an item for testing and, holding the covered part of the two loose wires, touch the free ends to the item. If the bulb goes on again, the item conducts electricity!

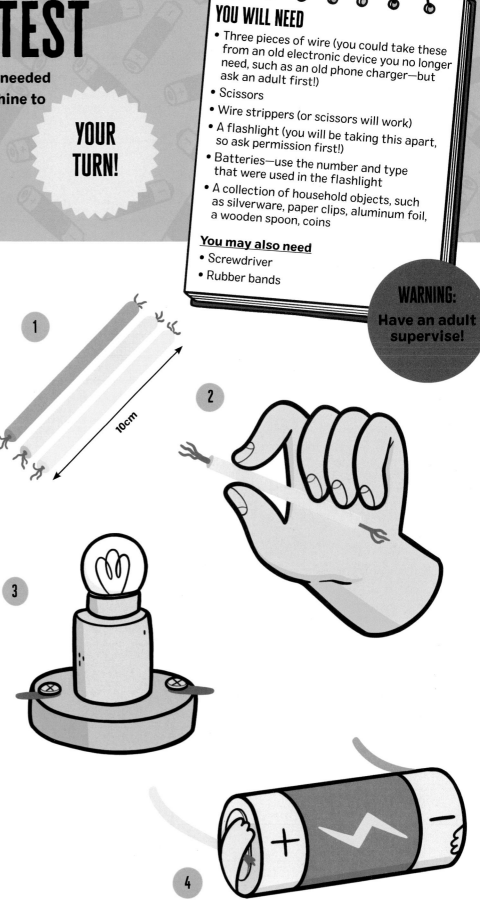

10cm

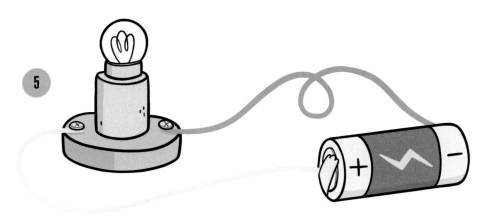

5

WHAT'S THE SCIENCE?

Electricity will only flow in a circuit. When you add material that conducts electricity to the circuit, the electricity can flow, turning on the light bulb. This material is called a conductor. Any material that does not conduct electricity will not complete the circuit and is called an insulator.

6

7

ANYTHING NOT WORKING? TRY THIS:

• Try reversing the way the wires connect from the battery to the bulb.

• Are the wires connected properly? Make sure the metal part is properly touching the connections on the battery and bulb. Try pinching them together with your fingers, or use clips to squeeze them together. Have you stripped back enough of the insulation?

• If the flashlight used two batteries but you have only connected one, try connecting the two batteries together end to end (the + end of one touching the – end of the other), and hold them together with rubber bands.

ELECTRICAL GHOSTS

Use this trick with static electricity to make cute little tissue paper ghosts that seem to fly by themselves!

YOU WILL NEED

- Scissors
- Tissue paper (Kleenex or toilet paper will do, but the lighter the paper the better)
- A pen
- A balloon

INSTRUCTIONS

1. Cut the tissue paper into circles of about 4 in. (10 cm) across. You don't have to be precise, but do make them roughly into circle shapes. You can make 3 or 4.

2. Put your thumb into the middle of the tissue paper circles and squish the paper around your thumb. When you take your thumb out, the tissue paper will look like a ghost.

3. Draw different faces on your ghosts!

4. Blow up the balloon and fasten it with a knot.

5. Rub the balloon on your hair or on a wool sweater for ten seconds.

6. Hold the balloon a few inches above the ghosts and see them fly up toward the balloon!

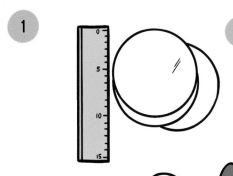

TAKE IT FURTHER

What else can you rub the balloon on to get the same effect? How many ghosts can one balloon lift at once? Can you lift more ghosts by making them out of different materials?

WHAT'S THE SCIENCE?

When you rubbed the balloon on your hair, the balloon built up a lot of negative charge, called static electricity. This charge then attracted the positive charge in the tissue paper, which is light enough to lift up and "fly" toward the balloon.

SEEING SOUND

Sound travels in waves. This neat experiment will help you see the patterns sound makes as well as hear it.

YOUR TURN!

YOU WILL NEED

- Bluetooth speaker and smartphone with Internet access
- Container big enough to fit the speaker/phone, such as a cake tin
- Tape
- Table salt (sea-salt crystals will not work as well)
- Plastic wrap (as an alternative, you could try using a colored balloon and cutting off its narrow end so that you can stretch the balloon over the container)

INSTRUCTIONS

1. Put your speaker inside the container.

2. Stretch plastic wrap over the top of the container and make sure it is smooth, with no ripples or saggy areas. Use tape to make sure the plastic wrap will stay in place.

3. Sprinkle table salt over the top of the plastic wrap. Spread it out roughly evenly, but don't worry about making it perfect—it will all move around soon anyway!

4. Find an online tone generator and play the sounds through the Bluetooth speaker. (Ask an adult to search for "tone generator.") Watch the salt move into a pattern as the sound vibrations invisibly wiggle the plastic wrap.

5. Try out different tones and see how the salt changes its patterns.

WHAT'S THE SCIENCE?

Sound is made from vibrations—through the air and through solid substances. Although you can't see the sound moving the plastic wrap, you can see the effect of those vibrations on the wrap by watching the salt "dance" on top of it.

1
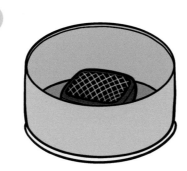

2
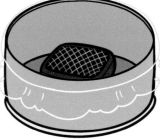

3

4
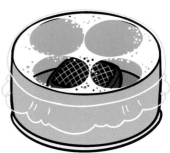

5

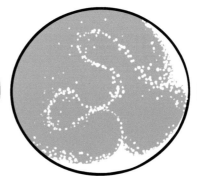
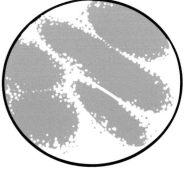

LEMON BATTERY

This battery, made from items found around the home, will power a small LED light or buzzer in an electric circuit. The voltage here is quite safe, but do not try to play with commercial batteries in the same way, as they can be dangerous.

YOU WILL NEED

- 1 or more lemons
- 1 zinc galvanized nail (a regular modern nail) per lemon
- 1 piece of copper wire or copper coin per lemon
- Sandpaper or vinegar
- LED light or buzzer component
- 3 to 5 alligator clips with wires

INSTRUCTIONS

1. Rub the sandpaper along the nail and copper wire/penny, to make sure their surfaces are "clean" of impurities. Alternatively, you could soak the penny in ordinary white vinegar for ten minutes. Rinse and dry it before using.

2. Bash the lemon around a bit—this helps break open the segments of juice inside.

3. Insert the copper wire/penny and zinc nail on opposite sides of the lemon. Push them in an inch or so (a few centimeters), but make sure they don't connect inside the lemon. The copper becomes the positive terminal of your circuit, and the zinc the negative terminal.

4. Use alligator clips to connect the copper to the longer, positive leg of the LED light, and the zinc to the shorter, negative leg of the LED light.

5. The LED should light up. If it doesn't, try switching the connections around, or you might need to add another lemon battery.

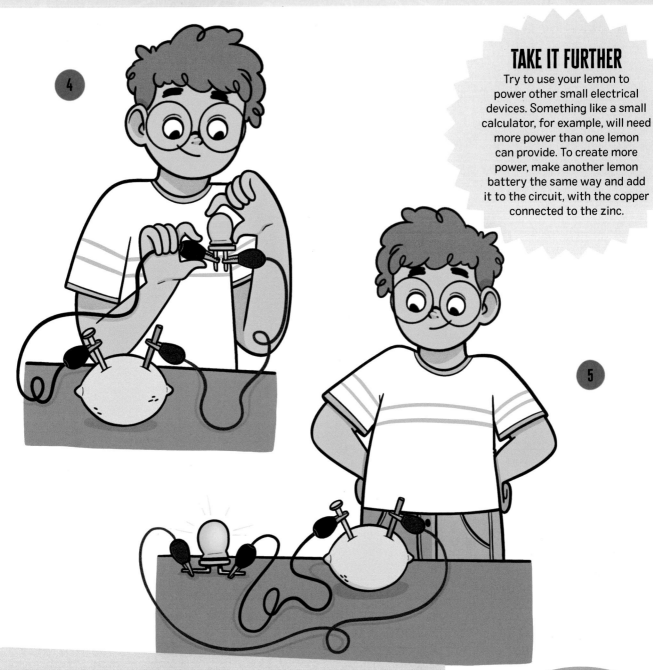

TAKE IT FURTHER

Try to use your lemon to power other small electrical devices. Something like a small calculator, for example, will need more power than one lemon can provide. To create more power, make another lemon battery the same way and add it to the circuit, with the copper connected to the zinc.

If you don't have . . .	Try . . .
A zinc nail	A strip of aluminum foil 1 in. (3 cm) wide by 8 in. (20 cm) long, folded into thirds lengthwise to make a strip of 1/3 in. (1 cm) by 8 in. (20 cm). You will need to ask an adult to use a sharp knife to cut a 1/3 in. (1 cm) slit in the lemon so you can insert the aluminum strip into it.
Copper wire	A copper penny, sanded down so it is nice and shiny
Alligator clips	Plastic-coated paper clips
Wire	A strip of aluminum foil as for the zinc nail, but rolled tighter to form something like a wire. Note that a foil wire does not have insulation, so you need to ensure the foil wire does not touch anything except for the parts of the circuit it is supposed to touch. If you touch it with your finger, it might feel tingly, but the voltage from a lemon battery is safe.

WHAT'S THE SCIENCE?

Batteries are made from two electrodes in a solution called an electrolyte. Here, the electrodes are the two different pieces of metal and the electrolyte is the lemon juice. The electrodes should be two different types of metal so that they react differently with the electrolyte. This difference is what helps generate the electricity.

GLOSSARY

Algorithm
A step-by-step way of solving a problem. Computers use algorithms to break down complex problems into smaller steps that are easier to solve.

Artificial Intelligence (AI)
The use of a computer or robot to complete tasks usually performed by humans.

Circuit
In electricity, the complete path around which electricity flows.

Conductor
A substance through which heat or an electrical current can flow.

Current
The flow of electricity from place to place.

Electrode
A conductor that carries electricty and touches the nonmetal part of a circuit.

Electrolyte
A substance that conducts electricity when dissolved in liquid.

Electromagentism
The magnetism produced by an electric current. Magnetism is created when electricity flows through metals.

Electron
A tiny particle, smaller than an atom. It is very energetic and spins fast around the center of the atom. Electricity is produced as electrons flow from atom to atom.

Fossil fuels
Energy-containing substance formed from remains of prehistoric plants or animals; coal, oil, or natural gas.

Insulator
A substance that does not conduct electricity or heat well.

Kinetic energy
The energy an object has due to its speed.

LED
A light-emitting diode. A device that emits light when an electric current flows through it.

Nanotechnology
Technology at the nano scale—which is measured in nanometers, or billionths of a meter—that is, things smaller than the width of your hair.

Network
In computing, a network is a group of computers linked to share information and resources. The network protocol means all connected devices follow the same set of rules.

Particle
Small units of matter. Atoms, molecules, and electrons are examples of particles.

Prototype
The first model of an idea that can be used to test how well it works and determine what improvements can be made.

Resistance
The ability of a substance to prevent or reduce the flow of an electrical current through it.

Supercomputer
A computer with a large memory that processes data much faster than a standard computer.

Turbine
A fanlike machine that catches the flow of water, air, or other gases and converts that motion into a fast spin.

Voltage
The pressure that sends electricity around a circuit. The bigger the currentand the resistance, the bigger the voltage.

Picture credits
The Publisher would like to thank the following for permission to reproduce their material.
8 Royal Institution of Great Britain/SPL; 14l ClassicStock / Alamy Stock Photo; 14br eclipse_images/istock; 23t dpa picture alliance / Alamy Stock Photo; 23b NurPhoto SRL / Alamy Stock Photo; 30 Lorado/istock; 31t D-Keine/istock; 31b AlasdairJames/istoc;k 39 Petmal/istock.

INDEX

THE AUTHOR & ILLUSTRATOR

JENNY JACOBY

Jenny writes and edits books and magazines for children. From writing science activity books to inspiring profiles, puzzles, and quizzes, she is passionate about making information fun. Jenny lives in London, England, with her family. Find out more at jennyjacoby.com.

LUNA VALENTINE

Luna Valentine is a Polish children's book illustrator living in Sheffield, England. She's inspired by science, and nature, and loves creating fun, lively characters who often get up to no good in their respective stories. When Luna's not drawing, it's only because one of her three pet rabbits has run off with her pencil.